Hiking
the
Clouds

The Journey to Mature Faith

JOËL MALM

MGPRESS

Hiking the Clouds: The Journey to Mature Faith
by Joël Malm

ISBN: 978-0-9985085-8-0

Author Photo Credit: James Dunworth

Table of Contents

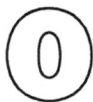

⓪
Waypoints

All theology that is vitally aware of its place in the true order of things, aspires to enter the cloud around the mountaintop where man may hope to meet the Living God.
— THOMAS MERTON

And we all, with unveiled face, beholding the glory of the Lord, are being transformed into the same image from one degree of glory to another. For this comes from the Lord who is the Spirit.
— 2 CORINTHIANS 3:18

The higher up a mountain you climb, the greater the likelihood you will find yourself hiking through clouds.

The same is true of faith.

When I was 12, I climbed my first mountain—a 12,000-foot volcano called *Agua* in Guatemala, Central America. As with most journeys in life, I was unprepared for what I would face. There was a storm, a mudslide, injuries, darkness, and limping home. By the time we reached the top, we were enveloped by clouds and couldn't see into the distance—only what was in front of us. It did not feel like victory. In many ways, it felt like defeat.

The journey of faith is much like climbing a mountain. It's slow and difficult. The higher you climb in your faith, the greater the likelihood you'll find yourself in a fog of questions, doubts, and uncertainty.

But there is a reward that comes with the journey of faith. He rewards those who seek him.

The reward is maturity. But the strange irony of maturity is: when you have it, you don't think you do. (Beware of anyone who tells you they are mature or enlightened.)

And yet, there are clear signs of maturity. The greatest of these is love.[1] "By this all people will know that you are my disciples, if you have love for one another."[2]

Love is the sign of mature faith. Love is what the Apostle Peter calls "the divine nature."[3] And the journey to love is endless. Because God is love. And God is endless.

You never arrive. It's a perpetual ascent, an unceasing evolution of your faith. Paul described it this way: "I press on toward the goal for the prize of the upward call of God in Christ Jesus."[4]

Growing in faith is an unfolding process. The ascent is infinite, but there are waypoints that reveal progress along the way.

> **Waypoint** *(noun)*: an intermediate point
> on a route or line of travel.[5]

This book is about the stages of growth in the life of faith. The journey goes by many names: discipleship, spiritual formation, sanctification. Whatever the name, this is the truth:

Spiritual growth happens in phases.

Typically, the process feels like three steps forward followed by two steps back. This is the nature of spiritual progress. Growth followed by what feels like retraction. It tends to be a slow process.

But the goal is to always be moving forward into experiencing more of who God is—growing in love.

True love for God and people exists in a space of total freedom—it cannot be forced. The life, death, and resurrection of Christ created the capacity for that freedom. The journey of faith is an ever-increasing awareness of the freedom that is already available to us. But to get there, we must shed layers of control, fear, and ego.

This is a lifelong process.

Kierkegaard observed, "Life must be lived forward, but it can only be understood looking backwards." You typically can't see progress in your spiritual walk until you look back.

This book is not a roadmap for growing in faith. It's more of a reflection on what growth looks like, looking back over the journey. It's descriptive, not prescriptive. It's a reflection on the journey of faith. I want to help you see that what you're experiencing right now—even if it feels like a crisis or low point—is actually part of the process.

I believe Peter laid out the stages in this journey of faith when he said:

> His divine power has granted to us all things that pertain to life and godliness, through the knowledge of him who called us to his own glory and excellence, For this very reason, make every effort to supplement your faith with virtue, and virtue with knowledge, and knowl-

edge with self-control, and self-control with steadfastness, and steadfastness with godliness, and godliness with brotherly affection, and brotherly affection with love. For if these qualitiesare yours and are increasing, they keep you from being ineffective or unfruitful in the knowledge of our Lord Jesus Christ.

— 2 PETER 1:3, 5-8

This sequence—from faith to agape love—are traits we should pursue throughout our faith journey. But, I believe God dedicates specific seasons for growth in each of these areas.

Each waypoint is foundational, building on the one before it. Some waypoints overlap. Once reached and embraced, every waypoint remains part of our growth forever. That's why we can't skip stages or rush the process. Each is essential for maturity.

We typically grasp only one level beyond our current stage. To those earlier in faith, the awareness of later stages can feel dangerous, even frightening—this is normal. The second half of faith feels very different from the beginning.

The sequence of waypoints Peter shares is the focus of this book. It reflects the journey I've seen many walk. It also reflects what I have experienced after forty plus years in the faith. This reflection may resonate with you, but if it doesn't, that's okay—we each experience God's work uniquely.

What I hope you take away is this:

Love is the sign of a mature faith.

The true measure for evaluating spiritual growth is: Have I come to love God and people more?

One warning. If you are new to the faith, there's a good chance this book will not resonate with you, yet. In fact, I discourage you from reading this book. In the early stages of any journey it's only natural to want to measure progress and speed. *Am I there yet?* This book is not for that purpose.

This book will best serve:

1 Seasoned believers who are navigating a shift in how they experience God and their relationship with him.

2 Those who are well into their own faith journey and serve as mentors, pastors, and counselors for those who are re-examining or wrestling with their faith. Incidentally, those best suited for that role tend to be…

3 Those who have been in the faith for years and have experienced disorientation or disillusionment with faith, but relate to the words of Peter when Jesus asked if he was going to leave him: "Lord, to whom shall we go? You have the words of eternal life..."[6]

If you've ever thought (or had the courage to say):

> *Faith isn't as simple as it used to be, but I'm in too deep to go anywhere else.*
>
> *God feels distant and silent lately.*
>
> *I'm not as certain about my faith as I used to be.*

Then welcome to the clouds.

Here's some good news: The clouds of faith don't mean you're lost—they mean you're climbing. They mean you're growing. If you'll stay on the journey, something beautiful is ahead.

During a crisis of faith, many look to other religions, believing Christianity lacks the depth and perspective they need. Please know this: You don't have to leave Christianity to find depth and a more open perspective. But you may need to move beyond the version of faith you were first handed.

The clouds are where you find that depth and perspective.

What you've experienced up to now in your faith is what you will need to navigate this new season. The goal is always to ascend to new heights and include what you've learned up to now.

Ascend and include.

The church offers lots of resources for folks in the first half of faith. But very few for those in the second. My hope is that this will be a resource for those in the second half of faith.

My goal is to help you reflect on the journey you've walked to this point and help you see that the next half of faith is going to be different from what you've experienced up to this point. And that's okay. It's part of the process.

One last thing.

They say anything worth doing is worth doing badly, at first. I'll be the first to admit that what I'm trying to explain here is a task beyond my ability. I'm going to do my best, but I might do it badly. I haven't arrived at some of the waypoints we'll be talking about. I wrote this book with much fear and trembling because I know that what I'm trying to explain is going to be misunderstood by many people I love. But I'm willing to take that risk (hoping those people will give me grace), because I know for many this will be a breath of fresh air that gives them the courage to continue in their faith journey.

I pray that as you reflect on your journey, evaluating and appreciating each stage, you'll gain a new-found hope and confidence that, "No eye has seen, no ear has heard, and no mind has imagined what God has prepared for those who love him."[7]

It's not over. Your faith isn't faltering. In fact, in many ways, it's just beginning. There are greater heights of faith ahead, even if you can't see where you're heading right now.

1
Faith

*The basis for any approach to self-transformation
is an ever-increasing awareness of reality
and the shedding of illusions.*

— *Erich Fromm*

*Now faith is the assurance of things hoped for,
the conviction of things not seen.*

— *Hebrews 11:1*

Faith is awareness.

More specifically...Faith is spiritual awareness that leads to alignment with reality.

True faith always transforms us in a way that allows us to embrace reality.

What reality, exactly?

The first reality is: *God is ultimate reality. And God is love.*

The second reality is: *"We are not human beings having a spiritual experience. We are spiritual beings having a human experience."*[8]

Faith is awakening to the spiritual reality of who God really is and who we really are—the greatest truth. When we awaken to this truth, we can love what *is* (reality) and see God's hand in all things.

Faith is about seeing with new eyes.

I don't remember exactly when I "got saved." As a pastor's kid, I raised my hand dozens of times in Sunday school, summer camp, and Sunday service. I'm sure it took somewhere in there. For me, coming to faith was a slow awakening. I just knew God was there and he was real.

For others, like my friend Marcus, the awakening was instant. He was high on drugs when a Jehovah's Witness came to his door and had him read a verse in Isaiah. He instantly became sober. He went straight to a Catholic church to find a priest—the only place he knew to go.

We come to faith when we're awakened to spiritual reality. We begin to see a bigger picture than just what is seen. It's not full awareness; it's a mustard seed. But that's enough to begin.

The Centurion, an outsider to the Hebrew faith, who asked Jesus to heal his servant exemplified this. Did he fully understand who Jesus was? Probably not. But he understood the kind of power he was dealing with in Jesus. "When Jesus heard this, he marveled and said to those who followed him, 'Truly, I tell you, with no one in Israel have I found such faith...'"[9]

When faith awakens us to spiritual reality, it naturally awakens a new perspective on physical reality.

Modern man has more awareness of physical reality than ever before. Our phones and artificial intelligence give seemingly limitless knowledge. A stream of news and information makes us aware of dangers to our health and physical safety. Early detection and prevention in medicine (a blessing in proper place), awareness campaigns, and global news heighten our consciousness of our physical vulnerability.

Physical awareness always leads to anxiety.

The moment Adam and Eve sinned, they became physically aware. "Then the eyes of both were opened, and they knew that they were naked. And they sewed fig leaves together and made themselves loincloths."[10]

Sin severed the awareness of the alignment and unity between spirit and body. It caused a dualistic division. We lost sight of the entire picture. A veil was placed between the two faces of reality.

"But when one turns to the Lord, the veil is removed."[11]

Faith awakens us and then leads us to re-align our lives around ultimate reality. It begins a journey of seeking God. "And without faith it is impossible to please him, for whoever would draw near to God must believe that he exists and that he rewards those who seek him."[12]

Faith has two components:

"Now faith is the assurance (ὑπόστασις, *hypostasis*) of things hoped for, the conviction (ἔλεγχος, *elenchos*) of things not seen"[13]

1   *Hypostasis (noun)*: Substance, assurance, confidence, essence, reality[14] (used in ancient times as a word for a title deed)

2   *Elenchos (noun)*: proof, conviction—evidence, reproof.

The two components of faith are: assurance and conviction. A mature faith holds both elements. I believe faith also has two distinct halves.

Assurance builds the foundation. *Conviction* takes faith to new heights.

Assurance builds confidence in God's authority. Like a title deed, it shows what is ours in Christ. *Conviction* internalizes that confidence and moves forward into the cloudy unknowns of the second half of faith.

Maslow and other psychologists showed humans move toward higher levels of spiritual awareness and meaning after lower, basic needs (food, safety, shelter) are met. God, the perfect father, knows this, and in the initial stages of spiritual awareness he proves himself by meeting physical needs—what seems most important to us. Many a Christian remembers the early days of faith when God answered their prayers in miraculous ways—the perfect parking spot in a full lot, the financial provision coming out of seemingly nowhere. He builds our assurance in faith by providing for physical needs.

But this is only the beginning of faith.

The second half of faith lives out of a deep inner conviction based on personal experience. Like Job confessed after his great trial: "I had heard of you by the hearing of the ear, but now my eye sees you..."[15] Jesus was getting at this when he asked Peter, "But who do *you* say that I am?"[16] [emphasis added]

At some point, the focus of our faith must shift into a higher kingdom awareness. This is why Jesus said: "Therefore do not be anxious, saying, 'What shall we eat?' or 'What shall we drink?' or 'What shall we wear?'...But seek first the kingdom of God and his righteousness, and all these things will be added to you."[17]

There is a natural progression God tends to use to move us into a mature faith. It comes in two stages.

The Two Halves of the Journey

Jacob spent the first half of his life deceiving, manipulating, and making deals to get a blessing. He made a deal with his brother to take his birthright blessing. He made a deal with his mother to con a blessing out of his father.[18]

In Jacob's first recorded encounter with God, God speaks to him from far off, up a ladder. He promises to bless him—the very thing Jacob has been desperately seeking. When Jacob awakens from his dream, he comes to an awareness of God's presence in his life. Immediately, in classic Jacob form, he makes a deal:

"If God will be with me and will keep me in this way that I go, and will give me bread to eat and clothing to wear, so that I come again to my father's house in peace, then the Lord shall be my God...and of all that you give me I will give a full tenth to you."[19]

This is a picture of the first half of faith. God comes to Jacob, awakens awareness, and Jacob responds as best as he knows how, from his old pattern of seeking a blessing to get his needs met.

God had already promised to give Jacob unmerited favor—he initiated the covenant. But Jacob felt the need to make a deal to ensure he'd be blessed. Essentially, he said *God, if you'll take care of me I'll follow you…. I'll even tithe."*

I know this kind of deal well. I made many with God in the early days of faith.

> *If you'll just give me —, I'll stop —.*

> *If you'll take away my struggle with —, I promise I'll start —.*

> *If you'll heal —, I'll —.*

When you feel limited and powerless as a child, you naturally make deals with those who have power. My 8-year-old daughter makes all sorts of "deals" trying to get me to give her what she wants. I won't give her what isn't good for her, but much of the time I want to give her those things anyway. She asks and I give them willingly, which naturally leads her to believe she has worked a deal with dad.

Early in faith, we tend to do the same. And God, just because he's cool like that, will often play along. We drum up our faith and pray, use the right words, declare with authority, and God answers. He provides. He heals. He gives. In this way, he builds our assurance in him. His faithfulness to give what we ask can offer the illusion that faith is all about what or how we believe.

But at some point, a mature faith requires a transformation.

The Blessing in the Wrestling

Jacob's deception, cowardice, and failures (all trying to get his needs met) all caught up with him later in life. As the pressure of his past mounts, God appears again. But this time, God comes very close.

As usual, Jacob begs for a blessing. He wrestles with him, trying to get the blessing he feels he needs. But God refuses. Instead, he wounds Jacob's hip and changes his name to Israel: *One who wrestles with God.*

Jacob only received his new identity after he wrestled with God and emerged with a limp. This is a picture of the second half of faith.

The second half of faith often begins with a struggle with God—a crisis that leaves us spiritually disoriented and carrying a wound for the rest of our journey. The wound looks different for each person—betrayal, failure, loss, abandonment, rejection, public humiliation, or a breakdown. Whatever its form, it leaves us less certain, less self-assured. That wound humbles us so we can grow in faith—not in our own strength, but in God's power.

In defeat and powerlessness, we discover the grace that matures us in love.

The shift into the second half of faith starts when illusions of control begin to shatter. We enter a season of wrestling with who God really is. It can feel like a crisis of faith or doubt. Often, it feels like we're actually physically dying. We step into what John of the Cross called a Dark Night of the Soul.

We enter the clouds.

We may feel less certain than we've ever felt about faith, but somehow in the wrestling, we have a deep sense of conviction—God is more real now than ever. But he is also more mysterious and bigger than we realized.

We begin to recognize some paradoxes of faith. Answers aren't as clear or as black-and-white as they used to be. From a place of greater awareness, we see that the biggest questions in life aren't problems to solve; they are tensions to manage. And we're ok with the uncertainty, because we are standing on the foundation built by the first half of faith.

This is a normal part of the process. The disorientation is to be expected if you're truly growing in faith. If we surrender to God's work in this next stage, we become free to love and be loved in a new way.

Ascend and Include

You get to the top of any mountain one step at a time, starting at the bottom. Every step of the journey of faith that Peter laid out: virtue, knowledge, self-control, endurance, godliness, brotherly affection, and agape is crucial for coming to mature faith. Each new stage builds on the last.

We don't despise earlier stages or resent their limited awareness; we recognize their foundational role in our transformation. The journey we had was the journey we needed. Maturity honors what was learned and has patience for those still walking earlier waypoints.

Those walking through the later stages of faith—endurance, godliness, brotherly affection, and agape—are often misunderstood by believers in earlier stages.

Their comfort with unknowing and openness to mystery may seem threatening or even heretical to those just starting the journey. The questions they wrestle with can feel unsettling to those new to the faith.

Because faith unfolds, we can only understand at our current level of awareness. In every stage of faith, God speaks to us at the level we understand, but he always calls us higher, beyond our current level of comfort and awareness. Humility is openness to the fact that there is always more. Stepping into greater awareness always requires a step-by-step process. We cannot skip ahead without missing something foundational for true transformation.

Each level awakens us to a new layer of truth. Truth sets us free, but first it must make us uncomfortable.

The price of growth is discomfort.

When we see something that is beyond our current level of awareness we tend to write it off as irrelevant or simply ignore it. We ignore the information because it is beyond what we can assimilate into our current framework of reality. This *ignore-ance*, is fine for a season, but eventually we must incorporate greater levels of awareness. We must grow.

Gregory of Nyssa boldly declared: "Sin happens whenever we refuse to keep growing."[20] This seems like an extreme statement, but the longer I live, the more I find it to be true. Paul emphasized the importance of growth when he said: "Therefore let us leave the elementary doctrine of Christ and go on to maturity..."[21]

We cannot keep circling the same spiritual ground at the base of the mountain and have a mature faith. We must climb higher. Maturity is perpetual ascent.

One of the most uncomfortable realities of greater awareness is that you can't go backwards. Once you've seen truth, you can't unsee it. The only real option is to press forward.

We naturally seek comfort, not growth. In words attributed to Nietzsche (a guy we don't quote much in church): "Most people are not seeking truth, they are seeking comfort in their illusions."

A constant climb can be tiring, so it's natural to have a "home" waypoint from the first half of faith we return to. Based on our temperament and history it's a comfortable and familiar place—some return to Virtue, others to Knowledge. My home stage is Self-control (which is why I spend so much time on it in this book). But these returns are only base camps for the climb ahead. We may pause to catch our breath, but we can't stay there.

Many great teachers have pointed out that, typically, the only thing that will move us into a new level of awareness is an experience of great love or great suffering.

Love and suffering lead to transformation. (And usually it's suffering.) Suffering wakes us up. It causes us to seek greater answers and awareness. Our salvation came through Jesus on the cross—the greatest image of love and suffering. The power of the cross and that sacrifice transforms us. If we remain open, God will use suffering to awaken us to new awareness of his grace. (Which is why the apostles talked at length about the power of rejoicing in suffering.)

Every stage of the journey takes us toward the end goal of loving God and others. To arrive at this full awareness, we must ascend and include all previous waypoints. No waypoint is more important than another. They all build on each other and require each other.

So let's explore the first waypoint of the journey of faith: Virtue.

1 VIRTUE

2

Virtue

*And the more I considered Christianity, the more
I found that while it had established a rule and
order, the chief aim of that order was to give
room for
good things to run wild.*
— G.K. CHESTERTON

If you love me, you will keep my commandments.
— JOHN 14:15

Every beginner must learn the fundamentals. Every
follower of Christ must do the same.

> **Fundament** *(noun)*: the foundation or
> basis of something.

Faith awakens us to the awareness that God exists, he created us, and we owe him our allegiance.
The immediate response to this awareness is a desire

to obey him and what he asks of us. We turn from our way (repent), accept the work of Christ on the cross, and begin the journey by bringing our actions in line with God's standards.

The first waypoint, Virtue, is about rules, standards, and laws that bring order and structure—a foundation of purity, righteousness, and living by God's expectations. Here, love is expressed through obedience to God's commands.

The greatest of these commands is: "Love the Lord your God with all your heart and with all your soul and with all your mind and with all your strength." And 'You shall love your neighbor as yourself.' There is no other commandment greater than these."[22]

Perfect love (Agape) is built on the foundation of obedience and virtue. We obey because God exists and he rewards those who seek him. The reward is love. So, ultimately, the reward is God himself—perfect love.

When I was 18, struggling with lust and sinful desires of every teenage boy, I was determined to live a life that honored God. I wanted to obey him completely. I wanted righteousness and holiness. I believed what I needed was rules. And monastic orders had them. Drawn to their vows of poverty, chastity, and obedience, I began spending time with the Franciscan brothers.

I was quickly disillusioned. They seemed unconcerned about the rules and way too filled with grace. I wanted strict discipline and sacrifice.

So I created my own rules: *I won't do that, I'll never go there.* I threw out any music that wasn't explicitly "Christian." I stayed away from people I thought were bad influences. But I regularly broke my own standards more quickly than I could lower them. I felt constant guilt. I often felt powerless to conquer my own desires.

Looking back, I realize the worst part was, when I managed to keep God's law I walked around with a feeling of superiority and arrogance.

Any desire for virtue that doesn't have love as its goal will always lead to self-righteousness.

"Now that you have purified yourselves by obeying the truth so that you have sincere love for each other, love one another deeply, from the heart."[23] Obedience to God's law prepares us to truly love God and others in God's way, rather than from our own misguided ideas.

There's nothing wrong with rules and laws, as long as they don't become an end in themselves. A healthy bit of legalism can keep you from unnecessary suffering that is caused by sin.

"The law of the Lord is perfect, reviving the soul...."[24]

When God was raising up Israel to be a great nation, he started by giving them the law. He promised:

> "And if you faithfully obey the voice of
> the Lord your God, being careful to do
> all his commandments that I command
> you today, the Lord your God will set
> you high above all the nations of the
> earth. And all these blessings shall come
> upon you and overtake you, if you obey
> the voice of the Lord your God."[25]

The law is a boundary that protects. It gives freedom within boundaries. When we know the parameters of where we can go and what we can do, it creates a sense of security. When boundaries are clear, it removes fear.

The Power of Boundaries

There's a classic study that involved a school built along a busy highway. When released for recess, students would all stay very close to the building, far from the highway. But as soon as a fence was built, the kids immediately began to explore the entire field—right up to the fence. The fence gave the kids confidence to explore.

We all crave the safety of boundaries. Kids and adults alike find security in them. Even when we push against them, their presence lets us run without fear, confident we're in the right place.

Chesterton put it this way: "And the more I considered Christianity, the more I found that while it had established a rule and order, the chief aim of that order was to give room for good things to run wild."[26]

Which is why Jesus said, "For this is the love of God, that we keep his commandments. And his commandments are not burdensome."[27]

The Law offers us freedom and clarity. It's a safe place to start growing.

"If you love me, you will keep my commandments."[28]

The foundational evidence that we love God is that we strive to keep his commands. There isn't much room for nuance. After all, a foundation should be solid, not flexible. These rules and boundaries help us learn to say no to ourselves and align ourselves with God's standards.

At this stage, black-and-white thinking offers structure, trust, and moral clarity—but it's only a starting point. Lasting growth calls for moving beyond rigid legalism toward wisdom anchored in love, the kind that can navigate life's deeper complexities.

That kind of wisdom, however, is built on a foundation of straightforward, clear-cut thinking—virtue.

In the best cases, virtue takes shape in childhood. A healthy, consistent home environment teaches impulse control, respect for authority, adherence to laws, and a sense of morality. It instills the value of right behavior. Ideally, that behavior is reinforced by affirmation and rewards that build confidence.

If you didn't gain this foundation early, you often have to learn it later in life—which is why many who come to faith as adults become intensely zealous. Having lived without boundaries, they swing hard toward rigidity, sometimes becoming overbearing with themselves and others. I've worked with many men who found faith in prison. Once released, their passion for rebuilding their lives often comes with a strictness that can feel inflexible. When you're laying a foundation of faith later in life, it's easy to overcompensate.

On the other end are those raised in strict, fundamentalist homes without a deep sense of grace. They may resent the rigidity, seeing it as stunting spiritual growth. But there is value in that structure—God's law shields us from needless suffering. Many who bear the scars of ignoring (or never learning) virtue envy the strict upbringing others reject, recognizing the pain it spared them.

Obedience to rules brings insight, and breaking them teaches through consequence. Artists innovate within artistic rules; scientists make discoveries by following the laws of their field. Faith works the same way—deeper understanding grows from a solid foundation of rules and standards. This is where wisdom in love begins.

Only the Beginning

My upbringing as a pastor's kid protected me from myself. I was taught Biblical principles and their value. I remember looking at others and wondering how they could make such foolish mistakes. Like Paul, in terms of living right, I was "beyond many of my own age among my people and was extremely zealous for the traditions of my fathers."[29] But this led to arrogance.

I remember sharing with my dad just how strong my desire was to live a righteous life. I said, "I want to be an example of living righteously so I can confront others about their sin without having any in my life."

Yes, I actually said that...

My father's response: "Let me know how that works out for you."

Virtue marks the starting point on the journey toward a true understanding of love. "If you love me, you will keep my commandments."[30] But obedience is only the beginning. As Thomas Merton pointed out, "The ability to choose between good and evil is the lowest limit of freedom, and the only thing that is free about it is the fact that we can still choose good."[31]

At the waypoint of Virtue, we align our actions with God's order, even without fully understanding why. Faith begins here, but it's not meant to end here. Staying too long risks legalism—where rules overshadow the spirit that gives them life.

Jesus rebuked the Pharisees for clinging to the letter of the law while neglecting the spirit of love. "Woe to you, scribes and Pharisees, hypocrites!...You blind guides, straining out a gnat and swallowing a camel!... So you also outwardly appear righteous to others, but within you are full of hypocrisy and lawlessness."[32] They missed the bigger picture, love.

You can do the right things, but without love for God and others, you become self-righteous. Today's "enlightened" age prizes compassion—something foreign before Jesus. The ethos of love has spread widely, even among non-believers, but without a foundation of virtue, true love becomes misguided.

Jumping to Agape without the earlier waypoints leads to what Paul warned Timothy about "…people will be lovers of self, lovers of money, proud, arrogant, abusive, disobedient to their parents, ungrateful.…reckless, swollen with conceit, lovers of pleasure rather than lovers of God, having the appearance of godliness, but denying its power."[33]

Some feel awakened and superior because they value compassion, yet they haven't built love on repentance, conversion, and obedience—on virtue.

Love not grounded in obedience to God's law is little more than virtue signaling. It may appear loving, but without a firm foundation, it carries no real power. Such "love" is self-righteous, unforgiving, blind to its flaws, and often controlling—measuring right and wrong by its own standards.

Without God's law as its root, love cannot mature into Agape; it becomes a false and harmful imitation.

Virtue is the foundation for mature faith which in turn results in mature love. But maturity requires that we not only know the rules, but we know why the rules exist. The next stage of the journey is a natural response for anyone with a desire to grow in their faith.

Enter knowledge.

NOTES FOR SPIRITUAL GUIDANCE

Just like the house doesn't resent the foundation, neither should you. This waypoint builds a foundation that will support rooms of grace, windows of wisdom, and a roof open to heaven. Embrace the restrictions and God's standards as freedom and protection.

FOCUS ON THE FOLLOWING

1 Trust the process, even if you don't understand it all. Embrace structure and rules as your friend.

2 Beware of pride and judging others—it's the potential danger of this stage.

3 Strive to live by the rules, but practice mercy for yourself and others who fall short.

2 KNOWLEDGE

VIRTUE

FAITH

3

Knowledge

Faith seeks understanding.
— ANSELM

*And it is my prayer that your love may abound
more and more, with knowledge and all
discernment, so that you may approve what is
excellent, and so be pure and blameless for the
day of Christ, filled with the fruit of righteousness
that comes through Jesus Christ, to the glory and
praise of God.*
— PHILIPPIANS 1:9-11

Awakened awareness naturally stirs a desire for deep-
er knowledge.

When love ignites genuine faith, it creates a
longing to know God more fully. The waypoint of
Knowledge is where we intentionally pursue greater
understanding of God—his will and his ways. Knowl-

edge and virtue tend to overlap, each reinforcing and strengthening the other.

My father was a pastor and I was surrounded by Biblical teaching throughout my life. Memorizing scripture was part of my school curriculum and I was raised in an environment that nurtured virtue. In my teenage years, when my faith became my own, I took full responsibility for my spiritual growth and embarked on a personal quest for deeper knowledge.

When the student is ready, the teacher appears.

The first time I heard Keith Lamb talk about God's sovereignty I was astounded. I didn't understand half of what he was saying, but he immediately expanded my view of God and his power. I don't know how I hadn't seen it before. It wasn't for lack of teaching. But a new level of awareness had opened my heart and mind to receive it. The Holy Spirit always leads us in truth as we're ready for it.

Peter said: "Make every effort to supplement your faith with virtue, and virtue with knowledge…"

At the waypoint of Knowledge, love takes the form of a desire to know God—the one we love—more deeply. We commit ourselves to studying the Bible and eagerly pursue learning. We're hungry for knowledge, so we seek a teacher.

A dear friend, a new Christian, quietly stepped away from the church where I was the teaching pastor and began attending another church. When I found out, I asked her why she had chosen the other church. She said. "They teach the Bible there. I need that right now."

Excuse me? I teach the Bible! I tried to stay calm. "What do you mean by that?"

She explained. "They teach me who the Amalekites were and where stuff is in the Bible." She wanted knowledge and Bible study tools that empowered her to better understand God's word. Our church offered this in small groups, but Sunday was primarily focused on outreach to a diverse group. I encouraged her to stay at that other church, as it was clearly what she needed right now.

At the waypoint of Knowledge, we become passionate seekers of truth. We gather information, study God's work in history, and learn creeds and doctrines to know why we believe and what God requires. Ideally, we also learn principles for applying this knowledge in love.

It's common to adopt theological frameworks—Calvinism, Arminianism, Pre- or Post-Tribulation eschatology—that provide certainty and shape our understanding. We often interpret faith through the lens of the system we embrace.

In early stages of faith, lacking personal experience, we rely on experts, traditions, and theology. We build our beliefs from what we learn from others. We attach to a teacher or mentor and trust their guidance exclusively, often dismissing anyone who interprets things differently: "He teaches the Bible. That other church doesn't!"

We're focused on making sure we have the right beliefs, the right theology. We feel the power of knowledge and we may even begin to feel mature.

But information is not necessarily transformation.

It's easy to confuse knowledge for maturity. But knowledge is only valuable if it leads to a growing love for God and others.

The Danger of Knowledge

During my awakening to knowledge, I remember thinking: *Why didn't anyone teach me this before? This is so important!* As I learned more about theology and Christian history, I felt frustrated with my upbringing, believing I hadn't been given the full picture. (A feeling I've heard many people express.)

In reality, the godly people who raised me had likely taught me, but we can only grasp what matches our current awareness, at most one waypoint beyond. Awareness comes when we're ready. I was ready to receive it now.

Along with this new understanding came frustration at what I saw as "bad theology" and widespread biblical ignorance. I became self-righteous, judging everyone (but myself) as having wrong beliefs.

There's a cognitive bias called the Dunning Kreuger Effect, "in which people wrongly overestimate their knowledge or ability in a specific area. This tends to occur because a lack of self-awareness prevents them from accurately assessing their own skills."[34]

A little knowledge can create a sense of power, but that power often breeds pride. When you know something, it's easy to forget what it was like not knowing. We begin to judge and condemn others who still don't know what they don't know.

The Apostle Paul said, "We know that 'We all possess knowledge.' But knowledge puffs up while love builds up."[35] (The King James version says, knowledge *puffeth up*, which I kind of like.) Humility is an accurate view of yourself. A little virtue and knowledge can blind us to our own failings.

The Pharisees had great virtue and knowledge, but their pride blinded them to the next stage in God's redemptive work that came through Christ. Jesus exposed the deeper issue that external virtue and knowledge alone cannot fix: "But I say to you that everyone who looks at a woman with lustful intent has already committed adultery with her in his heart."[36] You can obey all the rules, but still have a heart far from God's love.

Sin is more than your actions; it's your motives.

When we get stuck at the waypoint of Knowledge, believing it's maturity, we risk becoming what Jesus accused the Pharisees of being: *twice the child of hell.*[37] (Note the word *child.*) Knowledge is dangerous if not accompanied by increasing love and awareness of our own darkness, which easily hides behind our keeping of the rules externally while still having hearts with wrong motives.

I spoke at a men's event where all the participants seemed to have rock-solid Biblical knowledge. In a small group, one man started talking about how women must know "their place," citing chapter and verse. All the men nodded. His knowledge seemed exceptional, and he said it boldly. (Incidentally, I've found that most of what people say most confidently is actually them trying to convince themselves.)

Later, he mentioned his wife had threatened to leave unless he changed. He planned to bring her before the elders for discipline, rebuking her with scripture. What struck me was how much he knew of the Bible yet blamed his wife entirely, unable—or unwilling—to see his own part.

A great tragedy of our modern world is, we have made knowledge the highest aim. This is also true in the church. Many churches have developed amazing discipleship programs that focus on the waypoints of Virtue and Knowledge. We've taught the Word of God and given it the value it deserves. But like a student who graduates thinking they're fully prepared for life, some Christians believe they are mature disciples simply because they know the Bible and God's law.

But virtue and knowledge are literally just the beginning. They're only the foundation for what is ahead on the journey.

Awareness of truth should reveal areas within us needing transformation. Knowledge is meant to spark inner change, an authentic conviction rooted in personal faith, and ultimately serve as the starting point for the Holy Spirit's guidance.

"Anyone who listens to the word but does not do what it says is like someone who looks at his face in a mirror and, after looking at himself, goes away and immediately forgets what he looks like... But whoever looks intently into the perfect law that gives freedom, and continues in it—not forgetting what they have heard, but doing it—they will be blessed in what they do."[38]

Virtue and knowledge should eventually lead to living by the spirit of love.

When Nicodemus came to Jesus, sincerely seeking to understand, Jesus offered only this confusing statement: "That which is born of the flesh is flesh, and that which is born of the Spirit is spirit... The wind blows where it wishes, and you hear its sound, but you do not know where it comes from or where it goes. So it is with everyone who is born of the Spirit... Are you the teacher of Israel and yet you do not understand these things?"[39]

Nicodemus had virtue and knowledge. But Jesus was telling him he had to be born into a deeper, inner awareness of the Spirit. Only the Holy Spirit could bring this conviction of the unseen motives and motivations in his heart.

When we read God's Word, it reads us. The Holy Spirit uses scripture to reveal where we are out of alignment—but we must approach it with humility, or knowledge can feed pride.

Mature faith moves beyond formulas and dogma to rely on the Spirit's guidance. This requires internalizing truth at a deeper level—in our soul—and confronting our own darkness. Only the Holy Spirit can awaken this inner awareness, because most of us remain mysteries even to ourselves until that work begins.

King David acknowledged this reality when he said:

> *Search me, O God, and know my heart!*
> *Try me and know my thoughts!*
>
> *And see if there be any grievous way in me,*
> *and lead me in the way everlasting!*[40]

Every move to a new stage requires courage, but moving from knowledge to the next stage may require the greatest amount of it because it requires taking an honest look at what tends to scare us most—ourselves and our pain.

NOTES FOR SPIRITUAL GUIDANCE

Your roots are growing deep. But don't forget: roots exist to support the fruit. And fruit is always love for others. If the knowledge you gain doesn't lead to love for God and others, check your heart. Seek a mentor and study, pray, and focus on understanding.

FOCUS ON THE FOLLOWING

1 Feed your hunger for truth—but let love be your test of true understanding. (If knowledge of a truth doesn't make you more loving toward God and others, question your understanding of the truth.)

2 Beware of the pride that comes with being "right." Always recognize that truth has many layers and great nuance. We never fully understand the truth, not because the truth isn't true, but because our perception and motives are tainted.

3 Allow knowledge to open the door to self-examination.

3 SELF-CONTROL

KNOWLEDGE

VIRTUE

FAITH

4

Self-Control

*A humble knowledge of thyself is a surer way
to God than a deep search after learning.*
— THOMAS Á KEMPIS

*The purpose in a man's heart is like deep water,
but a man of understanding will draw it out.*
— PROVERBS 20:5-11

Discipline is destiny.

Lasting discipline comes not from willpower, but from uncovering the roots of our reactions and surrendering them to God's transforming power. Without humble self-awareness, we remain strangers to ourselves, captive to hidden forces that rule us. Discipline driven by self-awareness leads to self-control.

After college, I led backpacking teams around the world. During a four-month trip to China, I became acutely aware of my anger problem. I didn't like this about myself. I saw the damage it was doing to my relationships. I knew, "the anger of man does not produce the righteousness of God..."[41] I had memorized the verses and tried with all my willpower to beat it. But I could not.

After a major, explosive failure, a counselor helped me realize it was *my* problem, not the problem of those who were making me angry. I learned that anger and frustration are secondary emotions, responses rooted in fear. They were pointing to something inside me that I needed to surrender to God's love.

Facing my emotions and what they were trying to show me opened the door to a new stage on the journey. I began to see the deeper forces that were driving much of my anger, and for that matter, all my responses to the world around me.

The waypoint of Self-control brings awareness to the deeper aspects of ourselves. It's here that we confront the desires, thoughts, and emotions shaping our behavior.

In my experience, we reach this waypoint only through loss or failure—in a relationship, character, reputation, or self-control. The vulnerability and suffering strip away illusions, revealing our helplessness and awakening us to truths we'd never seen before about ourselves.

(Which is why, often, those who have struggled with an addiction have an easier time entering this waypoint. They've experienced their own powerlessness and self-destruction.)

It's only when we come face to face with our weakness and incapacity that we start to ask deeper questions. We begin to look for root causes.

Paul spoke about this dynamic in what is possibly the most relatable statement in the entire Bible. "I do not understand what I do. For what I want to do I do not do, but what I hate I do." But to him, there is no mystery to his actions. "And if I do what I do not want to do, I agree that the law is good. As it is, it is no longer myself who do it, but it is sin living in me..."[42]

The waypoints of Virtue and Knowledge awaken us to God's law, but that awareness alone can't free us from deeply rooted sin. True freedom comes through a deep inner work God wants to do in us. We must begin to identify the thoughts, desires, and emotions— the unseen parts of us—that hinder us from giving and receiving his love.

We don't see the world as it is; we see it as we are.

Sin veils our vision—distorting how we see ourselves, others, and reality itself. The work of Jesus removed the veil, "And we all, with unveiled face, beholding the glory of the Lord, are being transformed into the same image from one degree of glory to another. For this comes from the Lord who is the Spirit."[43]

Faith brings awareness that helps us see reality about ourselves. It reveals mindsets, beliefs, and wounds that impact our perspective on reality.

Which is why Paul said so emphatically, "Do not conform to the pattern of this world, but be transformed by the renewing of your mind."[44]

The Holy Spirit's sanctifying work frees us to see reality clearly, exposing the false identities, lies, and insecurities that block love. Embracing our true identity in Christ allows us to release the defenses and illusions that once defined us.

This requires a deep work in our soul.

Solomon said: "The purpose in a man's heart is like deep water, but a man of understanding will draw it out."[45]

Like a deep well, we have inner desires and motivations that drive how we interact with the world. We have past experiences and wounds that have impacted how we see reality. We have defense mechanisms and insecurities we use to protect ourselves from the wounds of sin in our fallen world. A wise person looks beyond his or her actions and draws out insight about the source of those actions.

A story is told of two men who are sitting by a river and hear a child calling for help, being washed downstream. They dive in and rescue the child. Then they hear another child calling for help in the river. They rescue that child as well. They hear another cry for help. One man jumps back in; the other begins running up the river bank.

The man in the river calls out: "Where are you going? We need to rescue these children!"

The man running upriver says: "I'm going upstream to figure out who is throwing these children in the river."

The waypoint of Self-control is going upstream to find the deeper source of our actions.

This requires looking at a part of ourselves we'd rather ignore: our pain. Which is why many refuse to move into this stage of faith.

Without confronting pain in our soul, self-control is about suppression, not transformation. Unprocessed or unacknowledged emotional pain (from sins we committed and those committed against us) leads to impulsive reactions—anger, addiction, avoidance, overreaction, or shutting down.

Real self-control isn't just about not doing bad things or knowing the right things to do—it's about transformation at the source. It's about recognizing what's underneath the urges and responses—fear, shame, rejection—and choosing a wiser, healthier response. Once we are healed, we don't have to strive to be loving, it just flows through us.

This is only possible if you're willing to look a little deeper at wounds that impact your motivations and responses.

Because facing ourselves is uncomfortable, many people never step into this waypoint. They get stuck in the Virtue and Knowledge stages. Virtue and knowledge (religion) can become an easy way to disguise our darkness and ignore our pain. But what we don't address in our thoughts, emotions, and desires will eventually show up in our actions.

Which is why loss and failure are so powerful (and helpful). They reveal our inability to conquer ingrained habits, sin, and addictions with willpower alone. We know the Bible and love God, but we still can't conquer our anger, our need for approval, the pornography, the alcohol. No amount of accountability or behavior modification seems enough to beat the dark side that constantly wants to emerge.

In this feeling of powerlessness, we're awakened to a need for something deeper.

The Deeper Work

I spoke at a men's conference where five speakers before me passionately scolded the men: "Stop sinning! Stop looking at porn! Stop lying!" Looking at the defeated, guilt-riddled faces of the attendees, I thought: *They're trying. That's why they gave time and money to be here.*

When my turn came to speak, I explained the need for inner transformation to precede outer transformation. I talked about the importance of looking at our soul motivations—our thoughts, desires, emotions, and past hurts that influence our responses. Afterward, the host made it clear he did not like what I had to say. He believed that willpower, not "psychology," is what these men were lacking in order to conquer sin. He was new to the faith and did not yet understand this truth:

Willpower alone is never enough to conquer ingrained sins and habits.

It's much easier to act like a Christian than to react like one. Our reactions in the physical always reveal what's in our soul. "A good man brings good things out of the good stored up in his heart, and an evil man brings evil things out of the evil stored up in his heart. For the mouth speaks what the heart is full of."[46]

What we *do* is always influenced by something happening inside of us. If you want to change your actions, you must recognize the forces driving those actions. Lasting transformation of our behavior always begins with inner transformation of our soul.

The unseen forces that impact our soul—past experiences and personality, nurture and nature—come together to create the complexity of who we are. And they must all be sanctified and brought into alignment with God's truth and reality.

To do this, we must face the reality of ourselves. We must explore the deeper parts of ourselves that are hindering our ability to give and receive love. We must learn to observe and recognize our thoughts and emotions and how they ultimately affect others and limit our ability to give and receive love.

In the waypoint of Self-control love looks (and feels) like vulnerability. Facing our wounds and emotions is frightening and uncomfortable to most, so many Christians never fully embrace this stage of inner transformation.

Some write off any thought of themselves as self-focus or self-absorption. But self-awareness is not self-absorption. Self-awareness is wisdom.

We cannot reach spiritual maturity without understanding our soul and its motivations. This is humility: seeing reality as it truly is. Carl Jung called it "shadow work"—acknowledging the parts of ourselves we've ignored or never seen. Jesus compared it to taking, "the log out of your own eye, and then you will see clearly to take the speck out of your brother's eye."[47]

Our soul contains the unseen parts of us that drive what we do.

The Greek word for soul is *psuche*. Psychology is the study of the human soul.

We are made in the image of God. This means that understanding people is a path to understanding God. Just like God is three parts, we have three distinct parts: *body, soul,* and *spirit*.

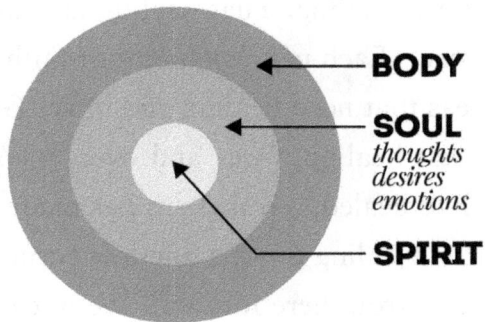

BODY

SOUL
thoughts
desires
emotions

SPIRIT

The Apostle Paul prayed, "Now may the God of peace himself sanctify you completely, and may your whole spirit and soul and body be kept blameless at the coming of our Lord Jesus Christ."[48] Sanctification is the process of getting all of who we are in alignment with God's work.

When we accept Christ, his Spirit brings our spirit to life. Then we begin the process of getting our thoughts, desires, and emotions (our soul), in line with God's Spirit. The natural result of this transformation is living by love in our actions (body).

Transformation of our actions and responses always starts by giving the Spirit of God within us free rein in our thoughts, desires, and emotions. We must remove what is hindering us from giving and receiving love.

This requires healing from the damage sin has caused in our thoughts, desires, and emotions. We all need healing. That healing is available because of Jesus.[49] Each new waypoint of faith opens us to new areas that need healing and offers God's grace to receive that healing. Over and over, Jesus told the people he had healed, "Your faith has made you well."[50]

Healing is not a onetime event; it's an ongoing process from here forward. We integrate ongoing healing into our journey as new layers of awareness reveal what needs to surrender to God's grace.

At this stage, discipleship turns inward. We discover wisdom in our God-given emotions, which expose areas still needing surrender. As we learn to give and receive love, we uncover wounds, defense mechanisms, and mental blocks that need healing.

We cannot do this alone.

Community is imperative in this process. We cannot figure out who we are apart from community. "As iron sharpens iron, so one person sharpens another."[51] We learn and grow in awareness by living with others.

Books and courses and personality profiles can help, but typically, this waypoint requires a guide—a counselor or spiritual advisor—who has done his or her own inner work. Anyone who has not, will struggle to understand the challenges that we face in this stage.

The Path to Inner Transformation

During my awakening to my anger and other emotions, I came across Richard Foster's Celebration of Discipline. He wrote, "The desperate need today is not for a greater number of intelligent people, or gifted people, but for deep people... God has given us the

Disciplines of the spiritual life as a means of receiving his grace... so that he can transform us."[52]

It revolutionized how I saw transformation. It helped me see that real change starts not with will-power, but with spiritual depth—from the inside out. Spiritual disciplines are the path to true self-control.

We don't practice spiritual discipline to please God, but to set ourselves free by building inner strength. True inner, spiritual strength naturally leads to out-ward freedom. When we have internal restraint, the external restraints are no longer necessary to keep us living in alignment with God's order.

In her teens, my sister once asked my dad, "When will I not have a curfew anymore?"

My father's response: "When you come in at a rea-sonable time you won't need a curfew." When you have internal restraint, you won't need external restraint.

Spiritual disciplines of prayer, solitude, worship, and fasting (and many, many others) offer inner free-dom through structure. They awaken us to the deeper parts of ourselves that God wants to transform.

Our false identities—what we do, what we have, who we know—are stripped away and we learn to be content in our identity as one loved by God. Free from much of the fear and insecurity that ruled us, we are able to see the gifts God placed in us for his glory and our fulfillment. This frees us to live out who we were made to be. We can truly walk in understanding that, "we are his workmanship, created in Christ Jesus for good works, which God prepared beforehand, that we should walk in them."[53]

This stage can feel so liberating and enlightening that it's easy to get stuck. Self-discovery can become addictive—one more personality test, spiritual gifts assessment, or self-help book promising to unlock what's holding you back. Many become hooked on the emotional high of healing, constantly chasing breakthroughs at conferences or in counseling. But we can't stay here. We must continue moving into greater awareness.

Our heightened self-awareness can cause us to become frustrated with those who seem out of touch with themselves or unwilling to face their emotions. The danger of awareness is it's easy to forget what it was like not having that awareness. True maturity is marked by patience for those in ealier stages—remembering we were once there too.

A defining mark of this waypoint is forgiveness. As we face the wounds that hinder our ability to give and receive love, we find freedom in releasing them. We acknowledge the damage of sin, yet choose healing, trusting God to turn even our wounds for his glory.

Forgiveness is not optional.[54] We must choose it. We cannot move forward into maturity without addressing our wounds and allowing God's love to heal us. Forgiveness purifies the deep waters of our soul and allows us to see clearly.

We forgive those who hurt us. We forgive the brokenness of the world. There's a crack in everything. Accepting reality as it is—not as we wish it were—is the path to freedom.

Forgiveness is not easy. Just ask Jesus. It cost him everything. But his love is what empowers us to forgive. Love always forgives.

(Note: Again, walking through forgiveness often requires a guide who has walked this path to help us.)

This decision to face our wounds and forgive is imperative preparation for the next stage of the journey. If you avoid or refuse this step, there's a slow closing down of the inner world. Until you're willing to look at your wounds—then choose forgiveness of self and others—you will be unable to proceed forward in maturity.

Soul-awareness is required to love others with wisdom.

NOTES FOR SPIRITUAL GUIDANCE

You're entering a stage many fear to approach, so be courageous. This stage can feel liberating, but it can also lead to self-centeredness. Prioritize soul-awareness, not self-improvement. Self-improvement will always be a result of allowing God's Spirit to transform your thoughts, desires, and emotions.

FOCUS ON THE FOLLOWING

1 Practice spiritual disciplines and let them shape you, but not shame you. Books by Dallas Willard and Richard Foster are helpful in this journey.

2 Find a wise guide (a pastor or counselor) who has done their own inner work and can guide you through greater soul-awareness and forgiveness.

3 Don't run from or ignore uncomfortable emotions, those too can be a gift that leads to greater connection with God.

ENDURANCE

SELF-CONTROL

KNOWLEDGE

VIRTUE

FAITH

5

Endurance

*The Dark Night of the Soul comes
just before revelation.
When everything is lost, and seems darkness,
then comes the new life and all that is needed.*
— JOSEPH CAMPBELL

"My God, my God, why have you forsaken me?"
— MATTHEW 27:46

It's only faith when you can't really see.

"Now faith is...the conviction of things not seen."[55]
The waypoint of endurance is where faith is truly
tested. Or perhaps, where deep faith truly begins. It's
where the clouds begin to roll in on the second half of
the journey of faith. Clarity can become elusive. The
climb gets very steep. We face a crisis of limitation
and powerlessness. Often, it feels like a crisis of faith.

What used to work no longer works. God may begin to seem silent.

Endurance is the stage of faith where certainty, control, and clarity begin to be stripped away, forcing us to surrender to God in the midst of darkness and disillusionment. Spiritual transformation comes through revelation and perseverance in the mystery.

It started for me on my birthday, early in my forties. I woke up with a distinct thought: *This is going to be the last year of your life.* That entire year, I was riddled with anxiety and a sense of impending doom. A friend suggested I had misunderstood the message to mean physical death. He felt it was the last year of the life I used to know. Looking back, he was correct, but I was certain I was going to die. I made it through that year, then wondered if the message meant the last *full* year. The weight hung over me like a dark cloud.

I pushed through the fear, best as I could. I took on a project that was far beyond my skill level and financial capacity. It nearly leveled me. A series of books I wrote didn't sell. I faced what seemed like one failure after another. A pandemic clipped my ability to escape the discomfort through travel. I'm fastidious about my health, but they found cancer, cut me open, and left a giant scar on my side.

It was chaos. Inside and out. My confidence disappeared. I wrestled with feelings about God that I had never had before. I felt abandoned by him. He seemed silent and uncaring about my suffering. The anger I thought I had beaten came back.

Friends gave all sorts of unhelpful and denigrating advice. "You have a wrong view of God! You need more faith!" Perhaps they were right. But I understood how Job must have felt when his friends gave their feedback about his trial. They just didn't understand.

At the waypoint of Endurance, God seems to take away all the structures that have supported our faith to this point—perfectly answered prayer, clarity, direction. We're forced to enter a dark cave empty-handed and alone.

In that cave, we wrestle with God. We wrestle with our beliefs about him. We come to see that God is not in our control. We call out to God, but he is quiet. We wonder if he has forgotten us. We feel wounded by him.

Many abandon the journey here.

And I don't blame them.

When prayers aren't answered, disappointment takes hold. When God seems silent, despair quickly sets in. When illusions of control are shattered, it can undermine our entire worldview. It often feels like dying.

The feelings can turn to frustration and disillusionment, even anger at God. As Teresa of Avila expressed during her struggle with feelings of God's absence: "God, if this is how you treat your friends, no wonder you have so few of them."[56]

Those feelings can bring guilt, "Am I allowed to feel this way about God?"

A crisis begins—a crisis of belief, a crisis of faith.

Those who abandon the journey here often go back down the mountain to a more familiar waypoint.

They try harder with more virtue.

They adopt a dogma or airtight theology that brings comfort—more knowledge!

They seek more inner healing and discipline—more self-control!

Some simply walk away from the journey.

Others feel betrayed. It's tempting to abandon the journey, but they're in too deep now. But they see no way of moving forward from here. Faith gets cloudy.

For those who embrace its discomfort, this stage is the beginning of an entirely new world of awareness. It's where deep faith is forged. It's where conviction truly begins. When all we can see is the next step in front of us, if that, we must endure with no assurance of what's ahead or where we're going.

This is hiking the clouds.

Onward Through the Fog

Mother Teresa spent her life serving the poor in India. She spoke with boldness and confidence about God's love to both powerful leaders and those who had nothing. But after her death, letters were shared where she expressed her own deep feelings of abandonment by God. "[But] as for me, the silence and the emptiness is so great, that I look and do not see, listen and do not hear–the tongue moves [in prayer] but does not speak…I want you to pray for me—that I let Him have [a] free hand."[57]

These words describe the clouds and the second half of faith. This new season of faith requires great perseverance and willingness to endure in the face of feeling like God is absent. The word the Apostle Peter uses for this stage—*hypomonēn*—means *perseverance, patience, steadfastness, or endurance*. I've chosen the word endurance for this book.

An endurance athlete who runs 100-mile races told me, "Being an endurance athlete just means you love pain." He was joking, but not really. Those who run the race for the long-haul must come to accept that pain is part of the journey. Jung said: "There is no coming to consciousness without pain."[58] The Apostles said: "we must suffer many hardships to enter the Kingdom of God."[59]

There seems to be no way around a season of feeling a sense of separation and great struggle for anyone who desires to be all God intended them to be. Even Jesus walked this path. He faced pain, discomfort, and even felt abandoned by God at one point. We must welcome the challenge of hitting a wall in our faith if we're going to grow into love.

Can we love God unconditionally, no matter what he does or doesn't do? Can we accept reality and what is, believing God is working his purposes?

In the suffering of God's silence and abandonment, we grow into a new level of strength. Perhaps for the first time, we develop true faith—one that doesn't depend on any outward evidence of God's presence. "We fix our eyes not on what is seen, but on what is unseen, since what is seen is temporary, but what is unseen is eternal."[60]

John of the Cross called this stage the Dark Night of the Soul. In the Dark Night, we wrestle with our complicated feelings of disappointment and disillusionment with God that we have suppressed up to this point. (Which is why the self-awareness gained in the previous stage is so important.) We must wrestle with God and be honest about our feelings about him.

"O Lord, you have deceived me, and I was deceived; you are stronger than I, and you have prevailed."[61]

These feelings and questions can feel irreverent or forbidden. *Are we allowed to be frustrated or angry with God?* (The answer is *yes,* as many Biblical heroes, including Jeremiah's quote above, show.) For those in earlier stages of faith, the questions we ask about God in this stage can feel sinful even to ask.

God will never do wrong to us. He only gives love. But we must allow the deep feelings to come to the surface and wrestle with them. Awareness of those feelings reveals areas of our life where we need to surrender.

Virtue, knowledge, and self-control offer certainty for belief. But now, inner experience based on that belief must become the guide. We must seek God in the darkness and confusion.

For those who arrive at this stage, there is no devotional book or class you can take to alleviate the discomfort. Even the best advice from mentors or guides can't fully give us what we need. At this point, we must understand:

There is no formula. There is only revelation.

There is no program, no discipleship handbook, and often no spiritual advisor who can give us answers. We must wrestle with God himself and listen to the inner guidance of the Holy Spirit in the darkness and uncertainty.

Seeking counsel from people who have not experienced their own Dark Night will render responses like Job's friends and leave us asking:

> *Did we do something wrong to cause this?*
> *Do I have unconfessed sin?*
> *Is this lack of belief?*

Searching your heart and motives is never a waste. And God doesn't mind our honest questions. But in the clouds, we have to surrender to the fact that this is part of the journey. Unknowing is to be expected.

If you *are* blessed with a guide in this stage, welcome their input. But also recognize their limits. They cannot be your source of strength. Only revelation from the Holy Spirit, guided by your foundation of virtue, knowledge, and self-control will move you forward. This is how we move from living by external guidance to living by rightly directed inner motivation, which leads to unconditional love.

We must trust the process and the preparation we have received in previous waypoints.

This has always been true. But we come to truly understand this reality in a deeper way at the waypoint of Endurance. We come to truly understand the nature of our relationship with God. He is God and we are not. We wrestle with this relationship.

This experience eventually leads to what John of the Cross calls *luminous darkness*. Nothing may change externally. In fact, you may feel more wounded and less certain, walking with a limp, but in your soul and spirit everything has changed. Your perspective has shifted and you have grown spiritually. On a deeper level, you understand and know that you, "have been crucified with Christ and I no longer live, but Christ lives in me. The life I now live in the body, I live by faith in the Son of God, who loved me and gave himself for me."[62]

This often feels like a faith apocalypse. Like your entire belief system is falling apart. *If I cannot ultimately control God, what do I have left?* This is perhaps the greatest mountain of faith that we must face. Surrender. But we start to realize that, yes, there are mountains that must be told to move. But in this stage, the mountain is you. Choose to surrender to God's work in the waypoint of Endurance.

Ultimately, we come to reframe God's silence as something we need to reach maturity.

When a teacher gives a test, they sit quietly in the corner while you prove you've internalized what you have been taught up to this point. We may raise our hands, seeking outside help, wanting to ask questions, but the teacher remains silent. The Dark Night, the waypoint of Endurance is a test. God's silence in the Dark Night of the Soul is not his disapproval; it's his confidence.

When we embrace the silence, we become stronger. For the first time, our faith isn't based on God's tangible evidence of himself. It's based on a deep inner awareness of his presence.

That inner awareness changes how we face and embrace all of reality. It opens us to an entirely new perspective. It allows us to surrender.

NOTES FOR SPIRITUAL GUIDANCE

Don't be afraid to wrestle with God and your feelings about him. Don't be afraid of your wounds. The wound you receive in the cave will be what prepares you for the rest of the journey. From the waypoint of Endurance onward, spiritual formation and discipleship will look completely different.

FOCUS ON THE FOLLOWING

1   Be honest about your doubts, disappointment, and disillusionment with God. Express those feelings to him. He can handle it.

2   Don't run from the discomfort or numb yourself. Be kind and patient with yourself. See this as an invitation to enter into a deeper understanding of God.

3   If possible, find someone who has gone through their own Dark Night to listen to you. But don't be surprised if many people simply don't understand the struggles or questions you're asking. They just don't understand.

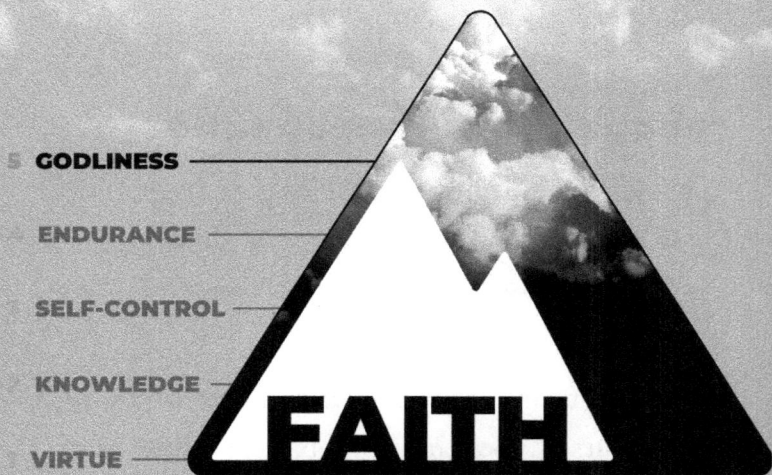

GODLINESS

ENDURANCE

SELF-CONTROL

KNOWLEDGE

VIRTUE

FAITH

6

Godliness

*The essence of surrender is getting out of
God's way so that He can do in us what
He also wants to do through us.*
— A.W. TOZER

*For we know in part and we prophesy in part,
but when the perfect comes, the partial will pass
away. When I was a child, I spoke like a child,
I thought like a child, I reasoned like a child.
When I became a man, I gave up childish ways.
For now we see in a mirror dimly, but then face
to face. Now I know in part; then I shall know
fully, even as I have been fully known.*
— 1 CORINTHIANS 13:1-12

Godliness is achieved by surrendering control and
embracing mystery.

At the waypoint of Godliness, we realize we are
empty and powerless. We allow the illusions of cer-

tainty and self to fall away—so we encounter God not through answers, but through trust, silence, and contemplation.

We are not in control. God is. As we truly surrender to him, we're no longer concerned about what's next. Instead we're focused on honoring what is. Reality, right here and now.

When you can love someone or something for everything it is, and isn't, (including reality itself) that is unconditional love. This allows us to be less concerned with perfection and, instead, be present in the moment. We find a unique contentment there, in the clouds.

"But godliness with contentment is great gain..."[63]

The Greek word both Peter and Paul used for godliness is *eusébeia* [εὐσέβεια]. The literal translation is "well-directed reverence."[64]

If the first half of faith is about building belief and seeking blessing from God; the second half is about reverence and respect for the fact that, ultimately, God's ways are mysterious and beyond our comprehension. We come to trust that he will bless us with exactly what we need, not what we think we need. We surrender to God's will, trusting that his plan for our life is what we would want our plan to be if we knew all the details.

We emerge from wrestling with God carrying a wound we will bear for life. It makes us feel limited, but in reality it has only shattered our illusions of control. The idols of understanding and clarity lie broken. Our motives are exposed, and we see how much of our faith has been driven by selfish desires and the need to be right. God is no longer a reflection of our ego.

God is more mysterious than we imagined—and even more unsettling, we discover we are a mystery to ourselves.

Only in this place of vulnerability and surrender are we open to a new way of seeing. Until we are convinced we don't have all the answers, we will avoid the discomfort of a new perspective.

Reality has much mystery. Mystery doesn't mean you can't understand it. It means it has infinite layers of understanding. You never fully grasp it, and there is always more to learn. This is humility. Only with humility—an accurate view of what is—can we see reality properly and embrace mystery.

Paul told Timothy: "Great indeed, we confess, is the mystery of godliness..."[65] Godliness is a *mysterion*, something you must be initiated into and experience on your own.[66] The first half of faith is initiation by belief and action, trusting the insight of creeds, theology, and advisors. The second half is faith through inner experience and contemplation. Only loss and letting go achieve this.

There are certain truths that can only be understood once we are crushed and weak—once we wrestle with God and walk away with a divine limp.

In my case, after the projects that crushed me, the surgery, and the failures, I stopped fighting and began to surrender. Sort of. I'm a fighter, so it doesn't come easily. But I'm slowly embracing life as it is—the mystery of God and his ways, the mystery of myself. I have more conviction than ever about my faith, but a much greater reverence for God's mysterious ways.

When we get to this place, we choose acceptance. Acceptance of reality. Acceptance of the bad, as well as the good. We begin to see God's hand in all things, despite the flaws, and find contentment in the middle of it.

In my case, I always had a plan for the future. After wondering if I was even going to live through my forties, I struggled to make long-term plans. In many domains of my life I still see no clear path forward, other than being in the present moment and making the most of it. It's humbling not to have a plan. (In fact, I hate it!) It's humbling to realize just how little

I understand about God and myself. But I'm slowly finding peace.

Surrender is the path forward into the clouds. The only other option is to double down on a previous stage, which many do. But to return to an earlier waypoint requires willful ignorance—a decision to ignore, rather than embrace, mystery. You can't really go backwards once you've seen deeper faith.

This seems to be part of what Paul addresses (in a much debated passage) when he said: "Therefore let us leave the elementary doctrine of Christ and go on to maturity... For it is impossible, in the case of those who have once been enlightened...then have fallen away, to restore them again to repentance..."[67]

Returning to a clearer and simplistic faith is appealing. To revert back to what you already know *for sure* is a promise of false security. You may find some comfort, but ultimately it will lead to discomfort. Once truth is seen it cannot be unseen.

Instead, we must "change and become like little children..."[68] We remain in a position of openness and wonder. Like a child experiencing the world for the first time, we must be open to learn without the biases of our past experiences and perspectives. We remain open to seeing God in new ways and surrender to a new perspective on God.

At the waypoint of Godliness love looks like surrender.

A.W. Tozer said: "The essence of surrender is getting out of God's way so he can do in us what he also wants to do through us."[69] Surrender comes from humility—a right perspective of ourselves and of God.

God is not who I thought he was and I am not who I thought I was. But I'm open and surrendered. This is humility. We move from a self-focused, "I will do this!" to "Let it be done unto me." We see that mature faith is a gift from God, not something we can develop on our own.

We let go of all-or-nothing thinking and begin to see God in all the pieces of our life. We come to acknowledge and embrace the paradoxes of faith. God is unknowable, yet infinitely knowable.

The Cloud of Unknowing

I was sitting in a group counseling session led by one of the most brilliant Christian psychiatrists I've ever met. He said something confusing to a woman who had just poured out her heart about a devastating loss she had experienced. The nebulous response he gave her frustrated me. "How does that help her deal with the pain of this?"

He smiled at me. "Joël, you always have to understand. Let the cloud pass over you, man. Let it surround you." (This book concept began in that moment.)

His answer explained nothing. But in some way, I got my answer. Sometimes we need to sit in the discomfort of lack of answers, trusting God. This is true faith. It's a deep confidence even when the answers aren't clear.

This may be the greatest message of the book of Job: God is a mystery, but he can be trusted. As G. K. Chesterton points out: "Indeed the Book of Job avowedly only answers mystery with mystery. Job is comforted with riddles; but he is comforted."[70]

The greater your faith, the greater your understanding that God is truly beyond human understanding. In the first half of faith, we come to know God through a sense of certainty. In the second half, we experience his ultimate unknowability. But with it, we find peace. Like King David, we can say: "My heart is not lifted up; my eyes are not raised too high; I do not occupy myself with things too great and too marvelous for me."[71]

Ancient fathers of the faith spoke of *apophatic spirituality* or *via negativa*—a focus on the mystery of God's unknowability, acknowledging that God is beyond all human concepts, images, and language. It's a process of unlearning by defining what he is not.

This is not agnosticism or giving up on searching. Instead, it's a deep knowing, a knowing through personal experience—the *mysterion*—without a need to explain or describe it. It's an inner authority.

Even using this language of "inner authority" can feel wrong or heretical to people in the first half of faith. After all, "The heart is deceitful above all things and beyond cure. Who can understand it?"[72] Inner authority sounds dangerous, but it is not dangerous if it is built on the previous stages.

This is where the first half of faith is imperative; it prepares us for the deep inner experience. Inner experience alone is dangerous and prone to self-deception. Apart from a foundation of faith in virtue, knowledge, and self-control (soul-awareness) we are prone to be led astray.

And yet, we also recognize that "the Spirit of him who raised Jesus from the dead dwells in you...."[73] Just before the passage about how prone we are to self-deception, Jeremiah speaks of the power of that

Spirit at work within us: "But blessed is the one who trusts in the Lord, whose confidence is in him."[74] Maturity in the faith builds a quiet and humble confidence in the inner voice of guidance.

Built on the foundations of the first half of faith, we come to trust the inner authority of the Holy Spirit. Reflecting Jesus' words to Nicodemus: "The wind blows where it wishes, and you hear its sound, but you do not know where it comes from or where it goes. So it is with everyone who is born of the Spirit."[75]

We are not slaves to the first waypoints of faith, but we will not abandon them. We choose to live in the tension. This is wisdom. This flexibility allows us to experience and embrace the infinite mystery of who God is.

"Oh, the depth of the riches and wisdom and knowledge of God! How unsearchable are his judgments and how inscrutable his ways!"[76]

Faith has many paradoxes. As Niels Bohr said: "The opposite of a correct statement is a false statement. But the opposite of a profound truth may well be another profound truth."

The greatest truths are *yes, and also*. God is transcendent (far off) and also immanent (very close). He is full of grace and also judgment (which, oddly enough, is also his grace). He is unknowable and also knowable on a profound, personal level.

The dualistic thinking of the first half of faith cannot handle these great paradoxes. But a mature faith is able to embrace great truth and live in the tension. Like the proverbial blind men describing an elephant, we know that any part of God we can explain is only a portion of the entire picture.

At this waypoint, you may find yourself without words to explain what's happening. Ineffable. Unspeakable. Or simply, "I don't know how to describe it." Because of this, often times, the most reverent response is silence. Words fall short. Prayer may look like embracing silence, rather than speaking and asking. Paul touched on this kind of experience when he said to, "...pray without ceasing."[77] I don't think he was talking about ongoing dialogue as much as ongoing awareness and experience of God's presence.

This is where contemplation begins. Prayer shifts from speaking to observing and listening. We are able to stand back and calmly watch, knowing God is working in all things. We simply seek his presence in the imperfection. He is there.

As we see with new perspective, there is a temptation to feel that traditional church no longer offers what we need. The fact is, a majority of believers in any church will always be in the early stages of faith. So, out of necessity, most churches focus on speaking to those in the first half of faith—simple messages with a nice bow on them, clarity about what that church believes is right doctrine. This message feels incomplete to us now.

Because there is no formula for growth in the second half, some believe they are "beyond church." But faith's goal is always greater love for God and people. People are the point. The moment we're tempted to separate from the church Christ died for is precisely the moment that our rich experience of walking in the faith becomes most needed in the body. "So I exhort the elders among you, as a fellow elder and a witness of the sufferings of Christ, as well as a partaker in the glory that is going to be revealed: shepherd the flock of God that is among you."[78]

Our witness and experience of the journey are most needed in the Christian community at the moment we are tempted to feel church no longer meets our spiritual needs. We have a responsibility to help those coming behind us on the journey. We are all growing. And we have a part to play in serving others on this journey.

We never outgrow the need for community. Even when we see the church's flaws, mature faith stays engaged with the Body of Christ. True love for the church comes when we see its shortcomings clearly, yet choose connection over separation. This is the nature of brotherly love. It loves people just as they are, but calls them to become all they could be.

Which leads to the next waypoint on the journey of faith.

NOTES FOR SPIRITUAL GUIDANCE

You are in sacred territory now—not because it's clear, but because it's clouded with holy mystery. What once was strong and structured is being undone, and that undoing is not your failure. It's your formation.

FOCUS ON THE FOLLOWING

1   Don't fight the mysteries of life, embrace them and seek to find God's presence in every reality of life.

2   Cultivate inner stillness, but do not separate from community. Your experience is needed by those in earlier stages of faith, but remember to be patient with them when they simply don't know what they don't know.

3   Don't rush to explain. Embrace paradox and discomfort as a path to hearing God's voice.

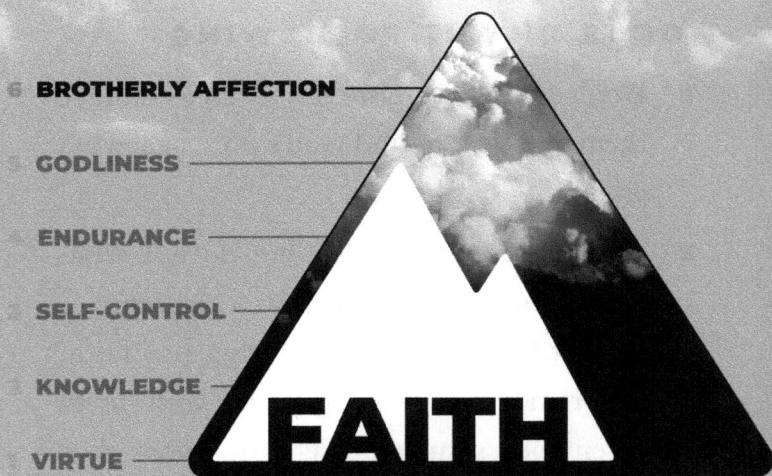

6 **BROTHERLY AFFECTION** ——

GODLINESS ——

ENDURANCE ——

SELF-CONTROL ——

KNOWLEDGE ——

VIRTUE ——

FAITH

7

Brotherly Affection

I really only love God as much as I love the person I love the least.
— DOROTHY DAY

We love because he first loved us. Whoever claims to love God yet hates a brother or sister is a liar. For whoever does not love their brother and sister, whom they have seen, cannot love God, whom they have not seen. And he has given us this command: Anyone who loves God must also love their brother and sister.
— 1 JOHN 4:19-20

Our love for others is the true measure of our love for God.

"He who does not love his brother whom he has seen cannot love God whom he has not seen."[79]

At the waypoint of Brotherly Affection, we begin to discover the deep interconnectedness of all people as members of one body in Christ. We are not separate. We are all connected in God's "love, which binds everything together in perfect harmony."[80] "We, though many, are one body in Christ, and individually members one of another."[81]

This mature, Christlike love is marked by empathy, detachment from ego-driven needs, and a willingness to suffer with others without being consumed by their pain. It flows not from a desire for validation, affirmation, or reciprocity, but from the abundance of God's love within us. As our ego is stripped away through earlier waypoints like Endurance and Godliness, our motives for love are purified, exposing how much of our "compassion" was often self-serving.

True brotherly love is not sentimental or performative; it's incarnational and sacrificial, seeing others as image-bearers of God and loving them without fear or need. This kind of love is not something we can manufacture—it is a gift formed in us through the journey of spiritual maturity, allowing us to love purely and patiently, like Christ does.

When I lived in a dangerous neighborhood in Mexico, I was shocked by how everyone seemed to be related. They all called each other *primo*, or cousin. I soon found this was not a reference to blood relation.

It's about the feeling of responsibility we have to look out for one another because we're all in this together. This is a picture of brotherly affection. Though we are individually responsible for ourselves in relationship to God, our connection to God's love compels a person of faith to, "look not only to his own interests, but also to the interests of others."[82]

I often wondered why Peter would make a distinction between two different kinds of love, *philadelphia* and *agape,* in his sequence. But after many years in the church, I've experienced that brothers and sisters in Christ are often the most difficult to love. Perhaps it's because we expect more from them or because we believe they should know better. But often, they are extremely difficult. Which is probably why the waypoint of Brotherly Affection precedes Agape.

If you can learn to love fellow Christians, you can love anyone. Which is why the church is the greatest testing ground for sanctification. You and Jesus may have it all figured out, but it's how you love others that proves it.

We are called to love others with pure love. We can only give this kind of love when we don't need them for affirmation of our own identity or for any need they can fill. We love them from a pure heart that God has given. We love them from God's own love flowing through us.

I make no claim to have arrived at this waypoint, yet. Though I want to. So, from this point on, I'll depend on the examples and stories of those who seem to have arrived at this place. Of course, Jesus is the place to start.

The Power of True Compassion

Over the years, I've served alongside many people who seemed to be extremely compassionate. They sacrificed time, money, and energy for others. Many served in full-time ministry. But I often saw that many of these compassionate people had a pattern of broken relationships. Those they had wounded all said the same thing: "They are some of the most loving people I've ever met, but I cannot be close to them." Many couldn't figure out how they had been so hurt by such loving people.

How was it possible that people with such good intentions, who sacrificed so much, could do so much relational harm to people? How can love turn into hurt so quickly?

This experience led me to question my own motives. *Why was I involved in ministry? Why did I want to do counseling?* If I was honest, many of my motives were self-serving. I wanted to serve God, but I also wanted the feelings of being a hero and someone who solved people's problems.

Brotherly affection is driven by pure motives. "Let love be genuine."[83]

Our tainted motives for love are nearly impossible to see until we've crossed many waypoints on the journey. Self-control, endurance, and godliness, when they've done their work, reveal just how misguided much of what we call love has been. We did it for approval. We did it for the expectation of reciprocity at a later time. (You care for me, I'll care for you.) We did it out of guilt. We did it wanting to be saviors.

Compassion is an obsession of modern man. Before Jesus, compassion was an unknown concept in our world. As Christ's teaching has influenced the world over two millennia, we've come to value compassion as one of the highest virtues, even among those who don't profess to be followers of Christ. But when compassion is separated from awareness that comes through the waypoints of the first half of faith, it will become destructive, "having the appearance of godliness, but denying its power."[84]

Much of what is called love is actually a selfish attempt to feed our ego through doing what's "right," virtue signaling, need for affirmation, or hoping to get our own needs met. Often, our compassionate expressions are driven by fear of not being accepted by society if we don't "care" like they say we should about any given issue.

Any act of love driven by anything short of God's love, built on the waypoints of the first half of faith, will only serve the purpose of feeding our ego. It leads to self-righteousness.

Brotherly affection is a gift of God. You can't will yourself into this kind of pure love. It is a gift that is given through growth on the journey of faith.

Jesus loved perfectly—seeing people for who they were and who they weren't, loving them even when they fell short. Rooted in his own identity and in the truth that each person is loved by God, he accepted them as they were while loving them toward who they could become.

When we can see people in their fullness—the good and the bad—and treat them the same, we love like Jesus. This kind of love is only possible when we are secure in our identity in Christ.

Jesus was deeply compassionate, but not consumed by human emotion or need. Just before the miracle of raising Lazarus from the dead, "Jesus wept."[85] He wasn't above entering into human suffering over loss, even though he was about to remove that suffering. Julian of Norwich reflected on this truth when she reportedly said, "Our Lord is so tender to us that He shares in our griefs even when He knows He will soon turn them into joy."

Brotherly love is empathetic, humble, and rooted in shared human experience. It is incarnational love—love that gets into the thick of the human condition but remains connected to the Divine Source of love.

Many great religious teachers speak of detachment, a word that can sound cold or stoic—especially to those new to faith. But mature love is the opposite of withdrawal. It is loving fully without letting desire, fear, or need distort that love.

Detachment is not disconnection; it is the freedom to love without fearing a person or depending on what they can give, because our needs are met in God. From this place, we can offer what is truly most loving. We simply become a conduit of God's love flowing through us.

We can only arrive at this kind of love after our ego has been crushed and stripped away in the dark cave of Endurance. When all need for validation, approval, and security from people is stripped away.

In his years of research into human need, Abraham Maslow discovered this truth: "Fully disinterested, desireless, objective and holistic perception of another human being becomes possible only when nothing is needed from him, only when *he* is not needed."[86]

You can only truly love a person when you do not need them, because the love you need is found in God alone. Only then can you love a person for what they need, rather than for what you receive.

This kind of love "is patient, love is kind. It does not envy, it does not boast, it is not proud. It does not dishonor others, it is not self-seeking, it is not easily angered, it keeps no record of wrongs."[87]

To love selflessly, we must release our need for others' validation and root our identity in Christ. This detachment offers presence and care without being ruled by desire or fear. It means caring deeply without clinging to outcomes—loving others as they are, while still calling them to grow.

You cannot truly love people until you no longer fear them. "There is no fear in love, but perfect love casts out fear."[88]

As long as we fear the emotional or physical harm others might cause, we are measuring their threat instead of loving them. When that fear is gone—trusting God to turn even harm to good—we can love sacrificially, as Jesus did.

Love rooted in Christ is calm and free, able to give what others truly need without being ruled by their need. It is fully present yet secure in its own identity in Christ—self removed, simply a conduit for God's love.

Jesus exemplified this. "But Jesus on his part did not entrust himself to them, because he knew all people and needed no one to bear witness about man, for he himself knew what was in man."[89]

People walking in this kind of love are realistic about the people they're serving. They accept them just as they are, while calling them to be more than they are now—like God loves us. Only when you can accept the person in their entirety, good and bad, can there be true connection with them.

At the waypoint of Brotherly Affection, we come to give and receive love from others as truly being part of a family—God's family. "The Spirit himself testifies with our spirit that we are God's children. Now if we are children, then we are heirs—heirs of God and co-heirs with Christ, provided we suffer with him in order that we may also be glorified with him."[90]

It's no accident that suffering is mentioned as part of this truth. The greatest suffering tends to be relational conflict with those close to us. Suffering and conflict in relationships are the true training ground for compassion, forgiveness, and community. We embrace the suffering that loving people requires because we know that, ultimately, loving people is loving God.

There is an inseparable connection between God's glory and the creation he has made. Our greatest expression of honor for God is loving people.

Proper love for people is always love for God. Which is where we begin to approach the perfect kind of love God offers.

Agape.

NOTES FOR SPIRITUAL GUIDANCE

True love, free from ego and fear, flows from our secure identity in God. As we're shaped by suffering and transformed by God's love, we learn to love people not for what they can give us, but simply because they are beloved by God. Brotherly affection is not something we can manufacture—it is a gift that emerges as we mature in faith and become conduits of divine love.

FOCUS ON THE FOLLOWING

1 Look for the image of God in those around you, especially those who are most difficult to love.

2 Pay attention to any resistance you feel in relationship to others. Ask God to reveal what he wants to teach you through the conflict.

3 As honestly as you can, evaluate where your motives for giving and loving others may be tainted.

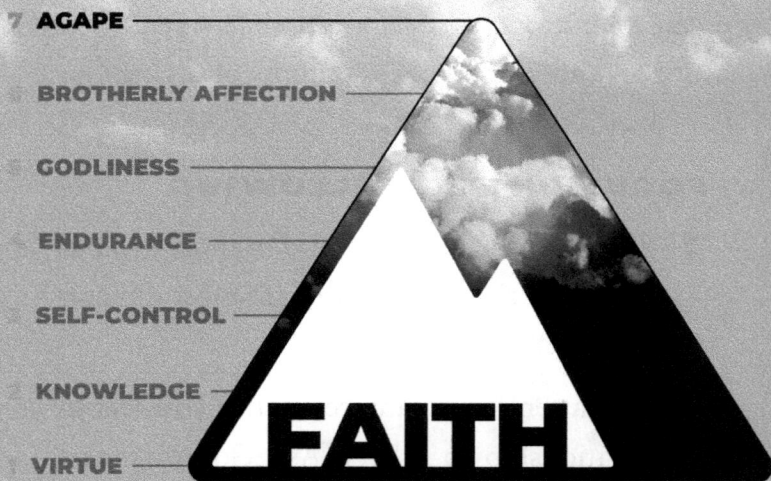

7 **AGAPE**

BROTHERLY AFFECTION

GODLINESS

ENDURANCE

SELF-CONTROL

KNOWLEDGE

VIRTUE

FAITH

8

Agape

*When one has once fully entered the realm of
love, the world—no matter how imperfect—
becomes rich and beautiful, it consists solely
of opportunities for love.*

— SØREN KIERKEGAARD

*Love is patient, love is kind. It does not envy,
it does not boast, it is not proud. It does not
dishonor others, it is not self-seeking, it is not
easily angered, it keeps no record of wrongs.
Love does not delight in evil but rejoices with the
truth. It always protects, always trusts, always
hopes, always perseveres. Love never fails.*

— 1 CORINTHIANS 13:4-8

By nature, God is perfect love.

As we grow in awareness and surrender to God's
love, that love flows through us and we "participate
in the divine nature, having escaped the corruption

in the world caused by evil desires."[91] With each way-point, we ascend and include each level of awareness and remove barriers to what is keeping us from giving and receiving love.

Faith awakens us to awareness that God's perfect love is the source and object of our life. All ego and self-focus are removed and we simply become conduits for his love flowing through us. It's a pure love. The pure in heart see God—in all things. They're able to love their enemies. They are able to love God and others unconditionally.

Every person of faith must walk this journey. Even Jesus was not spared having to walk this journey. "Although he was a son, he learned obedience through what he suffered. And being made perfect, he became a source of eternal salvation to all who obey him."[92]

The life of Jesus is the roadmap. Though he always embodied love, he still walked the journey of obedience through each waypoint.

He embraced the waypoints of Virtue and Knowledge, learning and following all aspects of the law.

His motives and desires, his human nature, were tested in the wilderness (Self-control).

He faced the Dark Night of Endurance on the cross. He wrestled with God's felt absence as he suffered.[93] But in that process, God was bringing salvation.

Ultimately, he was raised to life, revealing God's power to turn even the worst evil for his divine purposes—the power of perfect love.

When we trust that God is working all things for good, we lose the need to judge in the moment. His work is unfolding, and his hand is in everything. Whether events seem good or bad, caused or allowed, the outcome is the same—his love will conquer and turn all things for his purposes and our good.

This frees us to stop judging situations, others, and even ourselves, because the final outcome has not yet been revealed. When our needs are truly met in God, our perspective shifts. People and situations are no longer adversaries; we believe that all things work together for the good of those who love him. Even in the worst circumstances, God can fulfill his purposes.

We still name sin as sin and evil as evil, but we see them in light of what God can make of them. Like Paul, who said: "Therefore do not pronounce judgment before the time, before the Lord comes, who will bring to light the things now hidden in darkness and will disclose the purposes of the heart. Then each one will receive his commendation from God."[94]

Our awareness that there is spiritual reality behind all physical reality opens us to experience the Divine Union and connection in all things. "He is before all things, and in him all things hold together."[95] God is present, here and now.

This opens us to compassion, forgiveness, and a deep connection with God, freeing us to love others. Whatever we face, we trust his love. We see his hand in our lives and in history, his pattern from faith to love unfolding. Every waypoint was needed to shape who we are today.

In his love, he gave the law (Virtue and Knowledge)

In his love, he sent his Son to show us that obedience and knowledge aren't enough—we need transformation of our thoughts, desires, and emotions, our soul. (Self-control).

In his love, he allowed his Son to face the dark cave of abandonment by his father God, revealing the resurrection power that can come from death. (Endurance).

In his love, he sent the Holy Spirit to guide us into all truth (Godliness)

In his love, he revealed a higher standard: "A new commandment I give to you, that you love one another: just as I have loved you, you also are to love one another. By this all people will know that you are my disciples, if you have love for one another."[96] (Brotherly Affection)

God revealed truth to humanity in just the way we needed at just the time we needed it. He did the same for us, personally.

Seeing God's hand guiding all things, we embrace truth wherever it appears, knowing he is its source. Rooted in virtue, knowledge, and self-control, we can welcome truth even when partial or from unlikely sources, knowing it fits the bigger picture.

This awareness frees us to love others in the body of Christ at any stage of faith and to value churches and leaders focused on each stage of the journey.

Those who focus on righteousness and right living (Virtue)…

Others focus on sound theology and study (Knowledge)…

Churches and teachers that lead us to greater soul-awareness and healing (Self-control)…

Those focused on walking through wrestling with God, doubts, and hard questions. (Endurance)…

They're all necessary and all have their place in our spiritual growth. Because "we see in a mirror dimly,

[and] know in part..."[97] we recognize the limits of each focus, but value each expression of truth. "The important thing is that in every way, whether from false motives or true, Christ is preached."[98]

We love the body of Christ, no matter what stage of the journey those members are walking. We have grace and patience, remembering we were once at their same level of awareness.

From this place of openness, we become a resource for wisdom and mentorship to those in earlier stages of their faith. It's living with a deep confidence in God's work. This frees us to embrace the paradoxes and mysteries of life. It releases us from the need to label things with a dualistic framework.

Along with this, we accept ourselves in all our contradictions and flaws. We are vulnerable and open about our own struggles.

This is true spiritual maturity.

This kind of love is nothing we can create. It is a gift that is given. A gift that is available to us always, but the journey sets us free to walk in the fullness of this kind of love.

It leads to true freedom, which is always something inside of us, not outside of us.

As we come to a profound awareness of our position "in Christ" (a term Paul used over 150 times)—literally in union with him, we begin to love like he does. Can we walk in this kind of love at all times? I'm not sure. But we can certainly see glimpses of it. We recognize the many faces of real love when we see it.

The Faces of Agape

I have not arrived at Agape. On a good day, I see glimpses of it in my actions. But I cannot speak from personal experience of walking in this love (though I pray one day I can), so I must depend heavily on Paul's description of what Agape looks like:

Love is patient. We trust God's timing and processes. Not only in our life, but in the lives of others. We understand that we're all growing. We have patience with those at other stages of awareness, even if they are difficult or arrogant.

Love is kind. We accept others just as they are, but love them so much that we give of ourselves to help them grow into what they could be. But we do this gently and kindly. Just like the Holy Spirit, who gently leads us into new waypoints of awareness, we too are kind as we help others in their growth.

Love does not envy. We rejoice in the success of others, knowing that in Christ we are all connected. Their growth is part of our growth. We don't compare or envy. Envy is rooted in scarcity: if you have more, I must have less. Love lives from abundance—believing there's enough grace, favor, opportunity, and joy to go around.

Love does not boast, it is not proud. Agape doesn't need to be the center of attention. It's not self-promoting. It doesn't seek compliments or dominate conversations. Real love is rooted in humility. It listens more than it talks. It gives more than it takes. It is not fragile. It doesn't need to prove anything. It is secure, based in its personal experience of growth in God's love.

Love does not dishonor others. Agape never tears others down to build itself up. It doesn't participate in gossip, sarcasm, or belittling. It protects dignity—even when confronting wrongdoing. Love does not expose weakness for entertainment. It covers shame and restores honor.

Love is not self-seeking. Agape is other-focused. In a world obsessed with "me first," love says, "You go ahead." It sacrifices convenience and comfort for the sake of someone else's good. It doesn't manipulate or keep score. It doesn't love in order to get. It just gives.

Love is not easily angered. Agape has a long fuse. It's not touchy or defensive. It has nothing in itself to defend so it cannot be offended. It doesn't escalate minor irritations into relational breakdowns.

Love assumes the best. Agape does not take offense. It can hear hard truth without retreating into shame or blame. Knowing God is working all things for good, Agape looks past what it sees and looks for God's divine hand at work. Even in the worst situations, God is at work—we trust this.

Love keeps no record of wrongs. Agape forgives. When we remove the duality we use to judge situations—right/wrong, rigid thinking—we see that God even used the harm done to us to get us where we needed to be. Love chooses to remember with forgiveness. Not just once, but over and over.

Love rejoices with the truth. Agape and truth walk hand in hand. It doesn't avoid hard conversations or enable deception. Love tells the truth, even when it's painful, because truth leads to freedom. It celebrates honesty, growth, and authenticity. It wants what's best for the other person, even when it costs.

Love always protects, trusts, hopes, perseveres. Love is more than sentiment—it's commitment. Agape never gives up. It believes in redemption when others quit. It clings to hope in impossible situations. It protects people with presence and prayer and loyalty.

When we live from this kind of love, the entire world opens to us. Rather than becoming a threat, the world becomes a birthplace for rich sources of God's love. We begin to see that "In him we live and move and have our being."[99] God's love is the source of life and growth. "For from him and through him and to him are all things. To him be glory forever. Amen."[100]

Final Thoughts

Friends, you've climbed far. And like many who journey higher in faith, you may have reached the clouds—doubt, silence, restlessness, even disillusionment. These are not signs of failure but of movement and growth. If this book has done anything, I hope it reminded you that you're not alone in the fog. I hope it helped you reframe your journey, even the parts where you or others were misguided.

If you're growing in love for God and others, you're still on track.

Spiritual maturity is not mastery or arrival; it is love—deepening, widening, refining. Love that makes space for questions. Love that grows quieter, more courageous, more free. Love that mirrors the One who invites us ever upward.

As you move forward, may you carry gentleness toward your past, patience in your present, and hope for your future. The climb continues, but you're not lost—you are ascending. And the clouds, far from hiding God, are where he waits to meet you next.

Keep going. Keep trusting. The climb itself matures your faith, and the love awaiting at the summit is already finding its way into you with every upward step. "And I am sure of this, that he who began a good work in you will bring it to completion at the day of Jesus Christ."[101]

And we all, with unveiled face, beholding the glory of the Lord, are being transformed into the same image from one degree of glory to another. For this comes from the Lord who is the Spirit.

— 2 CORINTHIANS 3:18

Notes

1   1 Corinthians 13

2   John 13:35

3   2 Peter 1:4

4   Philippians 3:14

5   Waypoint: https://www.merriam-webster.com/dictionary/waypoint

6   John 6:68-29

7   1 Corinthians 2:9, NLT

8   Pierre Teilhard de Chardin is believed to have said this, but the quote is attributed to many spiritual directors.

9   Matthew 8:10

10 Genesis 3:7

11 2 Corinthians 3:16

12 Hebrews 11:6

13 Hebrews 11:1

14 Strong's Lexicon. 5287. *hupostasis* https://biblehub.com/greek/5287.htm

15 Job 42:5

16 Matthew 16:15

17 Matthew 6:31-33

18 Genesis 27

19 Genesis 20:22

[20] America Magazine.* (2011, January). Post-Christmas Spiritual Reading. America Magazine. Quote: "As Saint Gregory of Nyssa noted in the fourth century: 'Sin happens whenever we refuse to keep growing.'

[21] Hebrews 6:1

[22] Mark 12:29-31

[23] 1 Peter 1:22, NIV

[24] Psalm 19:7

[25] Deuteronomy 28:1-2

[26] Chesterton, G. K. (2001). Orthodoxy. San Francisco, CA: Ignatius Press. (Original work published 1908)

[27] 1 John 5:3

[28] John 14:15

[29] Galatians 1:14

[30] John 14:15

[31] Merton, Thomas. New Seeds of Contemplation, Merton, T. (2007). *New Directions*. (Original work published 1961) ch. 27 (1961).

[32] Matthew 23:23-24, 28

[33] 2 Timothy 3:2-5

[34] Dunning Kruger Effect. Psychology Today. https://www.psychologytoday.com/us/basics/dunning-kruger-effect. Accessed February 14, 2025

[35] 1 Corinthians 8:1, NIV

[36] Matthew 5:28

[37] Matthew 23:15

[38] James 1:25, NIV

[39] John 3:6-8, 10

40 Psalm 139:23-24

41 James 1:20

42 Romans 7:15-17, 20, 25b

43 2 Corinthians 3:18

44 Romans 12:2

45 Proverbs 20:5

46 Luke 6:45, NIV

47 Matthew 7:5

48 1 Thessalonians 5:23

49 Isaiah 53:5

50 Luke 8:48, 18:42 and Mark 5:34

51 Proverbs 27:17, NIV

52 Foster, Richard. J. (2002). Celebration of Discipline: The path to spiritual growth (20th anniversary ed.). HarperSanFrancisco. (Original work published 1978)

53 Ephesians 2:10

54 Matthew 6:15

55 Hebrews 11:1, ESV

56 Saint Teresa of Avila, The Interior Castle (Digireads. com Publishing, 2013), Kindle edition. Translated quote: "Ah, Lord, it is also on that account that Thou hast so few!"

57 Mother Teresa's Crisis of Faith | TIME. https://time. com/4126238/mother-teresas-crisis-of-faith/ Accessed April 7, 2025.

58 Jung, C. G. (1928). Contributions to analytical psychology (H. G. Baynes, Trans.). Harcourt, Brace & Company. P. 193

59 Acts 14:22, NLT

60 2 Corinthians 4:18, NIV

61 Jeremiah 20:7

62 Galatians 2:20, NIV

63 1 Timothy 6:6

64 Strong's New Testament 2150. ὐσέβεια https:// biblehub.com/greek/2150.htm

65 1 Timothy 3:16

66 Strong's Lexicon. 3466. mustérion. μυστήριον. https:// biblehub.com/greek/3466.htm. Accessed February 20, 2025

67 Hebrews 6:1-6

68 Matthew 18:3

69 Tozer, A. W. (2015). *The Root of the Righteous.* Moody Publishers. (Original work published 1955)

70 Chesterton, G. K. (2008). The Everlasting Man. Hendrickson Publishers. (Original work published 1925)

71 Psalm 131:1

72 Jeremiah 17:9, NIV

73 Romans 8:11

74 Jeremiah 17:7, NIV

75 John 3:8

76 Romans 11:33

77 1 Thessalonians 5:17

78 1 Peter 5:1-2

79 Romans 12:5 and 1 John 4:20

80 Colossians 3:14

81 Romans 12:5

82 Philippians 2:4

83 1 John 4:19

84 2 Timothy 3:5

85 John 11:35

86 Maslow, Abraham. "The Farther Reaches of Human Nature" (1971)

87 1 Corinthians 13:4-5

88 1 John 4:18

89 John 2:24-25,

90 Romans 8:16-17

91 2 Peter 1:4

92 Hebrews 5:8-9

93 Matthew 27:46

94 1 Corinthians 4:5

95 Colossians 1:17, NIV

96 John 13:34-35

97 1 Corinthians 13:12

98 Philippians 1:18, NIV

99 Acts 17:28

100 Romans 11:36

101 Philippians 1:6

MORE FROM JOËL MALM

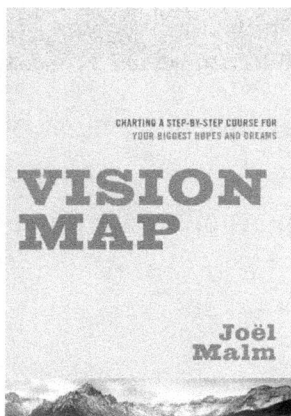

CHARTING A STEP-BY-STEP COURSE FOR
YOUR BIGGEST HOPES AND DREAMS

VISION MAP

Joël Malm

Is there a gap between you and your dream?

A few years back, Joël Malm had the idea to lead people on outdoor expeditions with a spiritual, God-centered focus. Following God's lead, he created a vision map, started his organization, and made it happen.

This book is a response to the question he often gets: *How do you do something like that?*

Whether you want to start a business, raise a family, run a marathon, plant a church, restore a relationship, or climb a mountain, you can take practical steps to see your vision come to be.

It's not a formula for overnight success, but it is a template to start anyone on the path to envisioning a God-given dream.

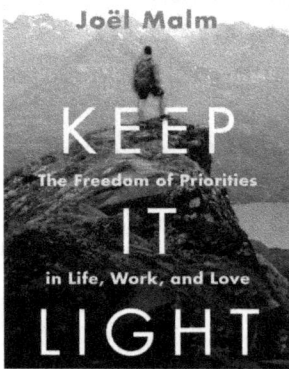

Overwhelmed? Tired? Feel like you can't keep up?

Jesus promises that His burden is light, but how many of us are actually feeling, well ... light? If life is like a long hike, most of us feel like we have a giant backpack of responsibilities and burdens that weigh us down and take the joy out of living. But Jesus offers another way.

Keep It Light will help you:

- ▲ Prioritize what deserves your time, money, and energy in this season of life

- ▲ Develop a plan to give your best to what matters most right now

- ▲ Balance the demands on your resources so there's time and energy for what you love most

- ▲ Create a stewardship plan to make sure that what God values is your highest priority

If the burden of life feels too heavy to handle, there's a good chance you're carrying something you weren't meant to carry alone.

www.ingramcontent.com/pod-product-compliance
Lightning Source LLC
Chambersburg PA
CBHW070812050426
42452CB00011B/2005